MINNESOTA

Photography by G. Alan Nelson

A BOOK OF 21 POSTCARDS

BROWNTROUT PUBLISHERS
SAN FRANCISCO • CALIFORNIA

BROWNTROUT PUBLISHERS

P.O. BOX 280070
SAN FRANCISCO • CALIFORNIA 94128-0070

ISBN: 1-56313-841-7
TITLE #: P6841

BROWNTROUT publishes a large line of calendars, photographic books, and postcard books.
Please write for more information.

Printed in Hong Kong

MINNESOTA
Bean Lake, Sawtooth Mountains, Tettegouche State Park

PUBLISHED BY BROWNTROUT • SAN FRANCISCO, CALIFORNIA

MINNESOTA
Lone oak, central Minnesota

PUBLISHED BY BROWNTROUT • SAN FRANCISCO, CALIFORNIA

MINNESOTA
The High Falls, Baptism River, Tettegouche State Park

PUBLISHED BY BROWNTROUT • SAN FRANCISCO, CALIFORNIA

MINNESOTA
Slough, Minnesota River, Big Stone National Wildlife Area

PUBLISHED BY BROWNTROUT • SAN FRANCISCO, CALIFORNIA

MINNESOTA
Glacial carved hills at Glacial Lakes State Park

PUBLISHED BY BROWNTROUT • SAN FRANCISCO, CALIFORNIA

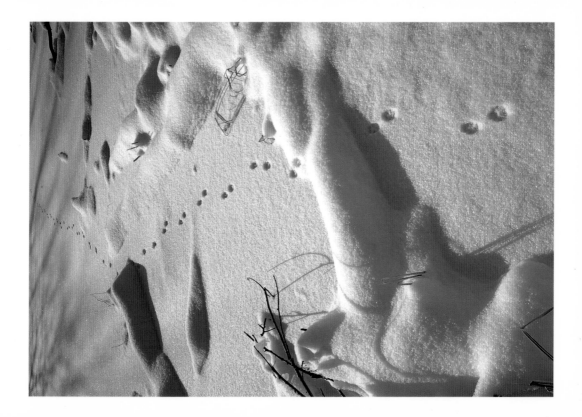

MINNESOTA

Fox tracks in fresh fallen snow, St. Croix River Valley

PUBLISHED BY BROWNTROUT • SAN FRANCISCO, CALIFORNIA

MINNESOTA
Norway pines and Lake Itasca, Mississippi River, Itasca State Park

PUBLISHED BY BROWNTROUT • SAN FRANCISCO, CALIFORNIA

MINNESOTA
Ferns on Wolf Creek, Banning State Park

PUBLISHED BY BROWNTROUT • SAN FRANCISCO, CALIFORNIA

MINNESOTA
Rocky shoreline of the Rainy River, Franz Jevne State Park

PUBLISHED BY BROWNTROUT • SAN FRANCISCO, CALIFORNIA

MINNESOTA
Red clouds over the infant Mississippi River, Crow Wing State Park

PUBLISHED BY BROWNTROUT • SAN FRANCISCO, CALIFORNIA

MINNESOTA

Lake Superior shoreline, Split Rock Lighthouse State Park

PUBLISHED BY BROWNTROUT • SAN FRANCISCO, CALIFORNIA

MINNESOTA
Aspens, north shore, Lake Superior, Tettegouche State Park

PUBLISHED BY BROWNTROUT • SAN FRANCISCO, CALIFORNIA

MINNESOTA
Minnehaha Falls, Minneapolis

PUBLISHED BY BROWNTROUT • SAN FRANCISCO, CALIFORNIA

MINNESOTA
White pines and fog, St. Croix National Scenic Riverway,
William O'Brien State Park

PUBLISHED BY BROWNTROUT • SAN FRANCISCO, CALIFORNIA

MINNESOTA
Twilight and full moon, Lake Superior ice floe

PUBLISHED BY BROWNTROUT • SAN FRANCISCO, CALIFORNIA

MINNESOTA
Waterfalls, St. Louis River, Jay Cooke State Park

PUBLISHED BY BROWNTROUT • SAN FRANCISCO, CALIFORNIA

MINNESOTA
Sundown, Lake Carlos State Park

PUBLISHED BY BROWNTROUT • SAN FRANCISCO, CALIFORNIA

MINNESOTA
Lake Lida, Otter Tail County

PUBLISHED BY BROWNTROUT • SAN FRANCISCO, CALIFORNIA